AF698817

The Hidden Power of You

An environmentally friendly book printed and bound in England by
www.printondemand-worldwide.com

Mixed Sources
Product group from well-managed forests, and other controlled sources
www.fsc.org Cert no. TT-COC-002641
© 1996 Forest Stewardship Council

PEFC Certified
This product is from sustainably managed forests and controlled sources
www.pefc.org
PEFC/16-33-415

This book is made entirely of chain-of-custody materials

First published 2012 by Fast-Print Publishing of Peterborough, England.

FastPrint Publishing

www.fast-print.net/store.php

The Hidden Power of You

Copyright © John Borthwick 2012

ISBN 978-178035-294-7

All rights reserved

No part of this book may be reproduced in any form by photocopying or any electronic or mechanical means, including information storage or retrieval systems, without permission in writing from both the copyright owner and the publisher of the book.

The right of John Borthwick to be identified as the author of this work has been asserted by him in accordance with the Copyright, Designs and Patents Act 1988 and any subsequent amendments thereto

A catalogue record for this book is available from the British Library

The Hidden Power of You

The art of turning doubts into success

by John H. Borthwick

Table of contents:

Page

4. Introduction
7. Your 'model' of success
9. The power of attitude
12. We learn to believe
22. The power of emotions
28. Promises, promises, promises
37. Who do you associate with?
40. Give yourself the winning edge
42. Your habits decide your future
46. It is later than you think
49. Failure is a great teacher
53. The only constant is change
56. The power of self-development
61. Persistence is omnipotent
65. Is good enough really good enough?
70. Know your behavioural quadrant
74. Do you listen to your self-talk?
77. The 'Garcia' effect
82. It's time to choose
86. Appendices

Disclaimer:

This book is not intended to give advice or make promises or guarantees, in any shape or form, that anyone following the ideas, tips, suggestions, techniques or strategies will have the same results as the people listed throughout the stories contained within the following pages or any other format this book may be published.

The purpose of this book is only to educate and inspire. The author, publisher and distributor(s) will not have any liability nor responsibility to anyone with respect to any loss or damage caused, or alleged to be caused, directly or indirectly, by the information contained in this book.

Introduction

We are only aware of successful people once they have become successful, in whichever form that success comes. It is very rare that we hear of the sacrifices and challenges that these people had to make or overcome. Onlookers tend to think this 'success' just happened organically, not realising the price that this individual had to pay to achieve what they achieved.

We all have challenges that we must overcome in order to succeed. Sadly, many people use these challenges as barriers to moving forward and striving for what they really want in life. Too many people are happy to accept mediocrity. The reason for this is that using excuses and blaming factors outside of their control is, for some people, easier; hence a more attractive option than these individuals taking responsibility for their own future.

During our time together I will share with you some stories. These will describe a very small number of the thousands of people who had major issues to deal with, but who did not allow these issues to get in the way of what they wanted to do. Ultimately, they found solutions instead of letting the issues become part of the problem.

All the examples I use are real examples, and have actually happened. I will also add some examples of experiences of my own. This is not to try to impress you but rather to explain and illustrate that each and every one of us has challenges. I am no different to anyone else, but because I was able to accept these challenges I took appropriate action to overcome them. This book is based upon a set of principles that others and I have followed, all of which I will share.

At the end of some chapters there are written exercises. The purpose of these is to help start the thought-process and to help you focus on where you want to go. It must be noted that these exercises are merely a starting point. For those who have some experience in these areas then I would ask that you use them as a refresher or aid-memoir. If you are new to these concepts then I trust they will give you a sound foundation on which to build an exciting and successful future.

It does not matter what your goals for the future are, nor does it matter what others think. The key point is that this future is yours, and yours alone. It takes just small steps, implemented consistently, and for you to give yourself sufficient time to acknowledge your accomplishments along your journey, in order for you to achieve your goals.

There are no guarantees in life and it would be wrong for anyone to try and suggest otherwise. However, if you work on the principles that are about to be explained it will tip the scales in your favour. Along the way, remember this: ***the only place success comes before work is in the dictionary.***

The ultimate objective of the following information and guidelines is to highlight that regardless of background, race, colour or sex; great things can be achieved if you have a strong enough desire to move forward and achieve more in life.

So let's take that first step into your exciting new future and let's enjoy the journey – I believe in you.

What is Your 'Model' of Success?

"Success is the progressive realisation of a worthy ideal" –Earl Nightingale

We live in a culture that tends to measure success based on how much money someone has accumulated or how many material possessions they own. This is misleading because success has different connotations depending on who you speak to; it is a subjective notion. For the purpose of this book, we will define success to be what your personal model of success is, **not** the model of success that society imposes.

If you deem your 'success' as becoming a head teacher, and you achieve that, then that is success. If it is to have two children and you do that then that is success. If your goal is to be a senior manager and you become a senior manager then that is success. If you want to own and run a café and be positively rated by customers and you do then that is success. If you work towards building a huge property empire and you achieve your goal then that is success. If you want to make £5 million in five years and you do then that is success.

In reality there are as many models of success as there are people dreaming of success. But the important thing is that you must be clear in your own mind what success means to you. I cannot stress this point strongly enough. If you are not clear on what success means to you, then how do you know what to aim for? As Earl Nightingale's quote above says: *"Success is the progressive realisation of a worthy ideal"*. This is probably the most accurate definition that I have heard of what success is, and you will note that it does not mention anything specific. The 'worthy ideal' can be whatever you want it to be.

The Power of Attitude

"Life is a grindstone. Whether it grinds us down or polishes us up depends on us" – L. Thomas Holdcroft

Of all the attributes we as humans can acquire and develop, the most important of these is a positive attitude. It is our attitude to whatever challenges we face that, ultimately, determines the outcome. We have a choice to react or respond to any circumstance, although we may not be able to control the events or the situations themselves. I am not saying that it will be easy, but the one thing we **can** control one hundred percent of all the time is our attitude. The ultimate question is whether we will react or respond?

The following story illustrates how much you can achieve by having a positive attitude. This story is about a man who lived through appalling conditions and treatment, and survived to tell his story in his book, entitled "Man's Search for Meaning". The author is Dr Viktor Frankl; who endured years in the Nazi Death camps, where his wife, mother, father and brother all died or were murdered in the gas chambers. Every single day the possibility of death hung over the prisoners' heads, as they suffered from hunger and brutality. Most people would say that it is impossible to control your attitude under such stresses. Dr Frankl approached the situation with the following:

"...Everything can be taken away from a man but one thing: the last of human freedoms – to choose one's own

attitude in any given set of circumstances, to choose one's own way.... in the final analysis it becomes clear that the sort of person the prisoner became was the result of an inner decision, and not the result of camp influences alone"

The likelihood is that most people will, fortunately, never have to endure what Dr Frankl and the other prisoners had to. My comment on this is that if even a few of those individuals experiencing such barbaric hunger and brutality could control their attitude then there is absolutely **no** excuse for us not to control ours.

Ultimately, it is your thoughts that determine the sort of attitude you have and how you project this to the outside world. Everything that happens to us is neutral. We then decide for ourselves what attitude we will adopt in any given situation, through the thoughts we have. So: we all need to control our thoughts. As William Shakespeare proposed:

"There is nothing either good or bad, but thinking makes it so".

When I carry out training, public speaking or coaching workshops, I share with my audience that once I had understood and practised the principles outlined in this book, things started to change for me. I wholeheartedly believe that because of these principles, I managed to achieve more in a five-year period that what I had previously achieved in twenty years. I have had my fair share of setbacks and failures, but the principles have always helped to bring me back on track.

As I also say during my workshops:

"The shortest distance between success and failure is the six inches between our ears. The sad thing is, for a lot of people this is the longest journey they will ever have to take".

We Learn to Believe

"Change your mental habits into belief instead of disbelief. In so doing, you bring everything into the realm of possibility" - Dr Norman Vincent Peale

Are your beliefs worth believing in? Most people would have no hesitation in answering this question with a resounding **yes**, and why shouldn't they? I must stress that I am not referring to anyone's religious beliefs. I am referring to people's beliefs in relation to their expectations and wants in their own lives. What do you believe you are capable of achieving?

If we look back throughout history, more often than not a person that has achieved a lot has not done so through intelligence, merit, or education alone, but through an unbreakable belief in what they were doing. They believed that what they wanted to achieve was possible, regardless of others around them doubting them, whether this be their friends or experts on the matter.

The following is an example of some people who I believe to have had unbreakable belief in themselves. One day in 1890, a very well respected bishop stated during a sermon:

"If God had meant man to fly, he would have given him wings".

That bishop was, in fact, the father of the Wright brothers, who 13 years later became the first people to succeed in flying heavier-than-air powered aircraft. It was fortunate for the world in which we live that the brothers chose to have unbreakable belief in themselves, and to continue in the pursuit of their dreams rather than listen to sceptics, including their father.

You may be fortunate enough to come across someone who will believe in you even before you start to believe in yourself. If you are fortunate enough to have an individual like this in your life; hang on to them. It will be this person who keeps you going. It is worth noting that this individual may not necessarily be someone already close to you such as a family member, loved one or friend.

I was very fortunate to have such a person in my life during my childhood, when I had a great desire to overcome a speech impediment I had. This person's name was Mr Millet. I received speech therapy until the age of eleven, and could not pronounce the word 'one' until the age of six. The first book I read by myself, at age fifteen, was "The House of Sixty Fathers'. At this time I still had my stutter, and subsequently everyone laughed when I told them I wanted to speak in front of people when I grew up. Mr Millet was different. He took me to one side and said:

"Don't let anyone tell you what you can or cannot do – especially when they haven't done it themselves. What do they know?"

These wise words have stayed with me ever since. I am now a trainer and a public speaker. (Incidentally it wasn't until I was in my late thirties that I was told I also have dyslexia.)

I will share with you another excellent example of the power of belief. For centuries it was widely believed that no human being would ever be able to run a mile in less than four minutes. Many people thought that the body would simply not be able to cope, and it would give up and the person would die. This widespread belief lasted until someone called Roger Bannister came along and changed this negative belief. In 1953 he broke the four-minute barrier.

But here is what is so amazing about Roger's achievement: within a month a number of other athletes managed to break the four-minute barrier too. What changed, you ask? The type of trainers they were wearing? Was the running track any different? Were they breathing different oxygen? NO! The only difference was that their belief changed, the belief now was that of, "if Rodger can do it then so can I".

In a similar vein, it may be worth your while to find a mentor who has achieved similar things to what you wish to achieve, and to emulate them. They may have already faced a lot of the challenges that you will face, and have first hand experience of overcoming these challenges. Your mentor can be the equivalent of what Roger Bannister was to the subsequent athletes who attempted to run a mile in under four minutes. Mentors are very important because they can serve to encourage and guide you, and help you avoid and overcome some of the pitfalls you may encounter.

In my experience, there are two particularly helpful aspects of having a mentor. Firstly, they can serve as an excellent springboard to bounce ideas off. Secondly, they will help you when you are struggling with your beliefs. Ultimately, they will believe in you even if you are finding it difficult to believe in yourself.

Here are some more examples of people who understood the power of belief, and came out a lot better off than those who doubted them.

Albert Einstein: Einstein dropped out of school at a young age and was profoundly dyslexic. When he explained the theory of relativity, which he believed was the true effect of gravity and not a force in itself, most people did not believe him. It was only after his death that Einstein was proven to be correct.

Evelyn Glennie: Glennie is arguably the world's best percussionist, yet no one would believe that she would be able to play her chosen musical instrument, let alone play it to the high standards that she does. This is because she is deaf and has been since the age of 12. Glennie is so good because she wholeheartedly believed she could be, despite her deafness. Interestingly enough, when playing with an orchestra, the way she 'hears' when it is her cue is to feel the vibrations through her feet. Furthermore, when 'listening' to music she puts speakers to different parts of her body.

Helen Keller: Keller is another amazing person who believed that she would inspire and help other people in a time when people with her condition were commonly put into asylums. Keller was deaf and blind, and could not speak due to an illness she had when she was young. Nevertheless, Keller inspired millions of people with the power of her beliefs and overcoming adversity. With the help of Anne Sullivan she slowly learned to write and speak and read with braille. Keller, to the astonishment of many, went on to write several books, to serve as a staff member of the American Overseas Blind Association and to speak in 25 different countries. Keller would not let herself be influenced by people telling her what she could or could not do; she believed in herself and found a way to achieve all that she wanted to. She said:

"To be blind, but worse is to have eyes and not see."

Sir Winston Churchill: Most people have heard of Churchill and of what he achieved in his life as the wartime leader, writer (for which he won the Noble Peace Prize for literature) and public speaker. What most people do not know is that Churchill had a lisp that challenged him in his speaking. He also suffered serious bouts of depression. Churchill warned the government of the impending dangers of Nazi Germany and no one would believe him, but because he had such great belief that his country was in danger he worked tirelessly to persuade the government of his belief, all whilst fighting his depression. In 1940 Churchill got his chance to really fight for his beliefs when he became Prime Minister. At the time many thought that he was not good enough for the role, and was the wrong person for the job, but he persevered nevertheless. Churchill said the following:

"Success is not final, failure is not fatal: it is the courage to continue that counts".

Sir Anthony Hopkins: Hopkins' story is one of what can happen when someone has a great belief in another person. Sir Anthony Hopkins, like so many other people of his young age, was told by his mother to get out from under her feet. He wandered down to the old theatre near where they lived, where there happened to be a rehearsal taking place. One of the actors had not turned up, and the director looked annoyed. Suddenly, the he caught sight of young Anthony sitting at the back. The director ordered:

"You boy, up here!"

Hopkins was given just one line to speak, but he delivered it with so much passion that the director said to him, "you will go a long way in drama young man." This was the first time someone had told the young Hopkins that he could be good at something, and it was this chance encounter that meant he started to believe in himself. Following this, Hopkins went on to be one of the most sought after actors in the world.

Pablo Picasso: Picasso was deemed to be a hopeless student because he would not learn mathematics, and at the age of ten he could hardly read or write. However, Picasso was to become a world-renowned painter whose works now sell for millions of pounds.

It is interesting to note that many people believe that once they reach a certain age then it is too late to try anything different, or they believe that they will not be able to achieve anything else. To illustrate how this could not be further from the truth, let's look again at Sir Winston Churchill, who was 65 years old when he became Prime Minister in 1940. Furthermore, Colonel Sanders, who is mentioned later in the book, was claiming his pension when he started Kentucky Fried Chicken (KFC), and even Ray Kroc was in his early 50's when he brought MacDonald's and turned it into the empire it became.

This poem from an unknown author puts this section into context:

Keep Believing in Yourself

There may be days when you get up in the morning and things
Aren't the way you had hoped they would be.
That's when you have to tell yourself that things will get better.

There are times that people disappoint you and let you down,
But those are the times when you must remind yourself
To trust your own judgments and opinions, and to keep yourself focused on believing in yourself and all that you are capable of.

There will be challenges to face and changes to make in you life,

And it is up to you to accept them.
Constantly keep yourself headed in the right direction for you.

It may not be easy at times, but in those times of struggle you will find a stronger sense of who you are. And you will also see your life in your own special way.

So when the days come that are filled with frustration and unexpected responsibilities, remember to believe in yourself.

Then all you want in life will be there, because the challenges and changes will only help you find the dreams
That you know are meant to come true for you

A lot of our beliefs come from what we have been told at school, by our family, from within our social circle, through self-talk and by the media. The previous examples are of people who chose not to believe what others said, but to question their words, and make it their mission to find out for themselves. The moral we can learn from this is:

Do not let someone else's opinion of you become your reality.

Ask yourself, are your beliefs worth believing in? If so then that's great. If not then perhaps a change is needed.

Ask yourself these questions on your beliefs about your path to success and your barriers to success:

What beliefs do you have that are particularly strong?

....

....

....

....

....

....

....

What other general beliefs do you have?

....

....

....

....

....

....

....

What beliefs do you want to hold on to and why?

....

....

....

....

....

....

....

....

....

....

What beliefs would you like to change or let go of?

....

....

....

....

....

....

....

....

....

Here are a few questions that you may wish to ask when deciding whether a particular belief is worth holding onto. Be honest with yourself here:

How does this belief help me?
Does this belief hold me back?
Do I want to change it?
Do I want to let it go?
What would be the benefits of letting it go or changing it?
What do I need to do to change this belief?
How has this belief influenced my life so far?
When do I want to get rid of this belief?
When do I want to start to change this belief pattern?
What <u>real</u> evidence do I have to back this belief up?
What am I going to do about it?

The Power of Emotions

"The ruling passion, be what it will, the ruling passion, conquers reason still" – Alexander Pope

Alexander Pope spoke the above line approximately three hundred years ago. Pope knew all about the power of emotion, in that we do not think based on logic, but on *emotion*, or 'ruling passion'. We may think that we are thinking logically but in reality it is emotion that is the primary driver of our thought processes. The extent of this will differ by individual, but is evident in everything that we do.

This fictitious story will illustrate this principle:

There was once a man who visited a village. Here he noticed that even though it was raining very heavily, everyone in the village was happy and joyous; no one was mourning, miserable or complaining about the weather. The man saw a café down a side street and thought he would take cover and have a break and have a drink of coffee to warm himself up. As he walked in he noticed for the second time that the atmosphere was upbeat and emotionally charged. He sensed that these villagers we very happy, and thought how wonderful it would be if he too could be that happy. Still wondering how he could achieve their level of happiness, the man walked up to the counter, ordered a drink and handed the cashier a five-pound note. When the cashier put the note in the till and did not hand the man any chance, he was outraged.

"Where is my change you swine!" he shouted.

The waiter calmly answered,

"Sir, you think and speak from your emotions. The change you so desire has to come from within. As you may have noticed, you are in the village named Happiness. The village of Happiness lies in the province of 'Emotions', and if you visit other villages in the province you will come across other examples of different emotions.

Emotions, if we do not control them, can cause adverse effects, and destroy all hope of achieving what we want. History is littered with examples of where this has happened. Alexander the Great and Adolf Hitler are two examples of many.

When emotions such as greed, envy and prejudice become our dominant emotions, these override our intellect, rendering disaster inevitable.

Make sure that you are in control of your emotions. Do not let then control you. Make them work *for* you, not against you.

Fear

The emotion that seems to have the greatest effect on many of us is fear. It is the most prominent obstacle that stands in the way of the path to success and fulfilment. It begs the question, how do we overcome our fear?

Firstly, we need to understand that fear is the emotion that makes people frightened about failure or rejection, and, in some cases, can make people fear success. We all have this emotion in varying forms and quantities, but what we also all have is the ability to overcome our fears and move forward. Too many people allow this emotion to paralyse them and some even use it as an excuse not to do something. *Fear will not be overcome by avoidance.*

To move forward and achieve our goals, we must learn how to manage our fear. The way to do this is not through bravado or denying the existence of the fear, but in being honest with yourself, facing your fear head-on and taking action to eliminate or significantly reduce it. Trying to avoid fear, or avoiding taking risks is called playing it safe. A useful analogy in explaining this concept to people is that not taking risks is similar to an aircraft staying on the ground because it is safe there. In reality, aircraft are not designed to stay on the ground; they are designed to fly. When you play it safe you are not actually beating your fear. In fact, you are allowing your fear to control your action and stifle your progress in achieving what it is you wish to achieve.

We should strive to understand what is causing us our fear, and use this as a springboard to break away from our self-inflicted prison of fear. We should not allow fear to act as an anchor around our necks that keeps us from moving forward. As Ralph Waldo Emerson put it:

"Do the thing you fear, and the death of fear is certain."

Worry

Let us briefly look at another emotion: worry. This emotion, if not managed, can cause people to be less productive than those who do not worry, or at the very least less than those who have this emotion under control. I am sure you will agree that worrying can absorb and waste a lot of your time, and if not of yours then of the people around you. The best way to deal with worry is simple and straightforward - go and do something productive.

People worry about a plethora of topics. For example, there are those who are worried about financial issues such as not being able to pay their bills, or being made redundant from their jobs. These worries are completely understandable, but worrying itself is not going to solve the problem. What *is* going to solve the problem is taking action and doing something about it. This could be something like upgrading your skills or taking control of your financial situation by seeking professional advice on money and debt management.

Finally, ask yourself this: how many times have you worried about something, then finally took action and had to ask yourself "what was I worried about?" If you are like me then this has happened many times. It is time to stop worrying.

Enthusiasm

The third emotion we will visit today is enthusiasm. Enthusiasm is an underlying emotion rather than something that is simply turned on and off like a light switch. It gives people the motivation and the incentive to achieve what they set out to do.

"*Nothing great was ever achieved without enthusiasm*".

This quotation was said by Ralph Waldo Emerson, and will ring true for many of you. I ask you to think of a time when you have achieved something. This may be completing a running race, teaching a child how to catch, delivering a killer presentation, or anything else you have experienced. Cast your mind back to the emotions you felt whilst you were working up to this achievement. Undoubtedly, one of these will have been enthusiasm. One of the characteristics of human nature is that everyday bumps and knocks to our confidence will have an adverse effect on our enthusiasm. These will limit our desire to attack the issues that are holding us back.

To keep hold of the emotion of enthusiasm, or get it back if it has diminished; take a moment to think of the things you are really passionate about. Write them down if that helps, and keep them somewhere you can see them every day. (Please also refer to my chapter on *persistence*).

I would like to leave this chapter on emotions with a quote by Golda Meir, who was the founder of the state of Israel and became their fourth Prime Minister. Meir tried to push forward a Middle Eastern peace agreement using diplomatic means, but was halted by the fourth Arab-Israeli war. When Meir resigned she remained active in trying to achieve peace. It was not until after her death in 1978 that it was revealed that she had been suffering with leukaemia for 12 years. The following is what Golda Meir said about enthusiasm:

"Trust yourself. Create the kind of self that you will be happy to live with all of your life. Make the most of yourself by fanning the tiny, inner sparks of possibility into flames of achievement".

Promises, Promises, Promises

"Obstacles are those frightful things you see when you take your eyes off your goal." **Henry Ford**

Out of all the great people who have ever written or spoken about the areas of self-development, success or achievement; there remains one theme that is consistent throughout. This is the importance of setting specific goals and deadlines.

So why is it that the vast majority of people fail to set themselves goals and deadlines? Is it that they simply don't know how to do it, despite the array of mainstream guidelines and examples? Are people too lazy? Are they too busy; is it to do with the task of goal setting itself that consumes valuable working time? Personally, it was only when the concept of goal setting was explained - on an audio programme by George Zaluke, in a subtle and almost sympathetic way, that I finally changed my own routine.

Since then I have discovered the concept explained in a different way. I wholeheartedly believe that if I had heard this many years ago when I first came across the idea of goal setting, it would have saved years of my 'drifting'.

This explanation, which I will share with you, came when I was working with a man known as 'The UK's Most Prolific Information Product Creator' – Peter Thomson, who shared an idea from Bill Bartman. This principle is so simple yet so incredibly profound. It really does have the prudential of changing your life and breaking through what may be holding you back.

Firstly let me ask you a question. When have you ever promised yourself something? This could be something that you want in the future, something for your loved ones, anything. More often than not you will do every thing possible to achieve what you have promised yourself, am I right? So, if this is true, why do people strive to achieve these 'promises' and not set the goals to achieve them?

Well, the answer lies in the word itself. **PROMISE.** There is something in our mental structure that compels us to try as hard as we can to keep these promises we have made to ourselves.

If, in the past, you have struggled with the concept of goal setting, for whatever reason; make one change. Change the words 'making goals' to 'making promises' and see what happens. Use 'making promises' whenever you acknowledge your aspirations, to yourself and to others around you. The likelihood is that you will compel yourself to commit to the promises you have made to yourself, because the one person you will not want to let down by breaking them, more than anyone else is... guess who? Yes, YOURSELF!

The importance of the promises you make to yourself:

- These promises will help to give you a sense of direction in life, they help in preventing you from being like a piece of driftwood in the sea of life; floating aimlessly with nowhere to be.

- These promises allow you to track your progress, and ensure you are on the way to achieving the results you want. It is worth mentioning that these promises that you have given yourself may, from time to time, become delayed. In this case, there are two things to remember. At worst, you will still be a lot closer to your objective by setting out this promise than if you did not. Secondly, you can always adjust the time frame if needed.

- Theses promises will make you feel better, improve your self-image and give you confidence, because you have something to strive for and you do not want to let yourself down.

- These promises are great for self-development: they will stretch you. You will discover areas that you may wish to develop for future accomplishments.

- These promises will give you focus and encourage you to seek clarity in all things you and others around you do. You will no longer settle for 'wishy-washy' statements and vague notions.

The importance of making promises and seeking clarity is illustrated in Lewis Carroll's Alice's Adventures in Wonderland. Here Alice is talking to the Cheshire Cat:

"Would you tell me please, which way I ought to go from here?"
"That depends a good deal on where you want to go," said the Cat
"I don't much care where –" said Alice
"Then it doesn't matter which way you go" said the Cat

So, use the template overleaf to write your promises down over short, medium and long terms. Enjoy yourself in doing this exercise. Ensure to describe them in detail and be specific with what your promise is and *why* you want to keep this promise to yourself. The answer to the *why* will indicate how sincere you are about the promises themselves. If you are not sincere about why you want to achieve something then do not promise that you will achieve it. Instead, prioritise those that are closest to your true passion and desire.

Exercise one – Identifying your wants and desires

Given the chance to make 'promises' (i.e. goals) to yourself regarding all the things that you want to achieve and accomplish in life, what would these promises be? Write down the top ten and take care not to overthink the exercise, just enjoy the exercise of day dreaming!

1)..

....

2)..

....

3)..

....

4)..

....

5)..

....

6)..

....

7)..

....

8)..

....

9)..
....

10)..
....

Exercise two – The following are the six questions that you must ask of each of your chosen wants and desires

To start getting into gear and to set the wheels in motion so you can move towards keeping these promises to yourself, ask yourself these important questions and write the answers down. Work with your most important three first, and then move on to the next objectives, and so on.

What is it specifically that you want to achieve or accomplish?

Why do you want to keep this promise to yourself?

How will you accomplish this promise?

What date do you expect to have completed this promise to yourself?

Where are you now in relation to where you want to be?

Who can and will help you in achieving your objective?

Exercise three – Identifying your strengths, weaknesses, opportunities and threats (SWOT analysis).

Select the number one promise that you want to keep, and perform this SWOT analysis. This will give you a quick and effective analysis of the promise that you want to keep for yourself. It will also help with identifying what needs to be worked on and what to be aware of along the way (then repeat the process for each of the promises).

Strengths...
....
....
....
....
....

Weaknesses...
....
....
....
....
....

Opportunities..
....
....
....
....
....

Threats..
....
....
....
....

Who Do You Associate With?

"Birds of a feather flock together" – Anonymous

We must never underestimate the power of association, because the people who you associate with will have a direct effect on your future achievements. It has been said that your income will reflect the average income of the five people you associate with most. This principle does not only apply to income; the five people with who you associate with most will also affect the way you dress, walk, conduct yourself, and will even influence the way you talk, the words you speak and your attitude to life.

Do this little exercise when you next see any of the five people you spend the most time with. Take a mental note of how they are dressed, how they talk, and their outlook on life; are they mostly positive or negative? (You may already have an idea of their income). Then, when you are alone, compare these features of your associates with those of with your own. You will almost certainly find that there are many similarities. This need not shock you, because we as humans tend to gravitate towards people who are similar to us. The most challenging question to ask yourself is: 'Are these people helping me towards the promises I have made to myself, or are they holding me back?'

Only you will know this answer. Be honest with yourself. If you find that you are being held back, you may need to find the courage to leave your comfort zone and seek alternative people to associate with, people who will stimulate you, and help you towards your promises. I appreciate that this is not easy to do, but sometimes it has to be done so that you may progress at the rate you wish to. Speaking from my own experience, I made the decision to reduce the time I spent with one particular individual who I had known for over 15 years. This was not easy, but I have never looked back since I saw the positive changes in my attitude and spirit.

It is important that I stress that I am not suggesting for one moment that you have to cut these people out of your life completely. It may be that a small reduction in the time you spend with then is enough to reduce the negative effect they may have on you. Assess your feelings during and after your time with these people. Do you feel motivated, optimistic and driven? Or do you feel drained, lethargic and pessimistic?

Think of your closest associates right now. Are these people living the kind of life you want, or are they more successful than you? Where are they likely to be in five or ten years? Are they standing still or moving towards the promises that they have made for themselves?

When you are with these people, what are typical conversation topics? Do your interactions tend to focus on looking back in the past (not to be misunderstood – it is great to share happy past experiences from time to time) or where you are going in the future? Are the conversations that you have based on taking responsibility, and how you can enhance your future, or do you blame external factors? Ultimately do your interactions tend to be forward looking or backward looking?

I'm sure we've all heard the saying *"you are known by the company you keep".* Be aware of whom you associate with – it is your choice and your choice alone, so choose wisely.

Give Yourself the Winning Edge

"Be not afraid of going slowly: be afraid only of standing still"- Chinese proverb

So what is the 'winning edge'? It is so small, so obvious, and yet so subtle. Most people either fail to see it, or deem it as insignificant and therefore unimportant. In reality, this edge is what separates those who keep their promises to themselves and those who do not.

The 'winning edge' concept is constantly demonstrated in nature. An example of this comes in the form of a flower that grows all over the world, named the water hyacinth. For argument's sake, let us say the pond that it is introduced to measures twenty square feet, and is fairly still. On day one, the plant can hardly be seen. After two weeks it will have reproduced to cover an area of approximately one square foot. At week three the plant will only have covered an area of about six feet by three feet. Then on day twenty-nine the water hyacinth will have covered half of the pond, and on day thirty (just twenty-four hours later) the pond will be totally covered by the water hyacinth.

The water hyacinth's takeover of a pond demonstrates a compound effect. It shows the effect of a small action, carried out every day, in nearing us to our objectives, and eventually producing massive results and delivering our promises.

The small steps that you take on a consistent and persistent basis will gradually drive you closer to keeping your promises. At first it may look as if nothing is happening, and this is where most people give up. But if you continue to make incremental changes and advancements, soon enough you will see how you are keeping that promise to yourself. Before long, the wall will be breached and the floodgates will open.

This, the concept I have just explained, is the winning edge. It is what the people who fulfil their promises understand; that in order to move towards their objectives, they must get into the habit of doing something on a consistent, persistent basis. How do you eat an elephant? You do it by taking one bite at a time. That is the power of the compound effect and the winning edge.

Music teachers always say it is better to practice a little bit every day than for hours on only one day per week. Similarly, ensure that you are putting the time in each and every day to achieve, do not have a spurt on one day and neglect the rest.

"I will walk with anyone who wants to walk, I will run with anyone who wants to run, but I will not stand still for anyone" Anonymous.

Your Habits Decide your Future

"People do not decide their future. They decide their habits…and their habits decide their future" – Anonymous

We all have many habits. Some of them will be good and some not so good. The interesting thing is that we are all born without any habits whatsoever. So what is it that causes us to develop these seemingly harmless habits?

Our habits are formed by the many hours that we have spent performing the same actions. They are formed by the routines that we have carried out, to the point that we have subconsciously 'programmed' them into our mind, and they now require no conscious thought process.

It is only when you are actively aware of your habits that you can make the decision: to change or embrace? Are your habits an asset or a liability? Are they holding you back or driving you forward?

Because our habits become so ingrained in our mind over time, they can be very difficult to break. Here is the good news: ALL habits can be broken if you are determined and serious enough to do what it takes to break them. But, a word of warning, some habits will take longer and be harder to break than others.

It has been said that it takes thirty days to create or break a habit. However, if, for whatever reason, you fall short of your intentions within this thirty-day process, the whole process starts again. Now, I cannot confirm whether or not this is an exact science, but let me share with you a personal example of the habit-breaking process that took me roughly fifty days.

In 1994 I noticed that every day I watched the TV for about two hours. The programmes I watched were not of any real significance to me, and these two hours fell at roughly the same time every day. It was a habit. So I decided that I would break this habit. I stuck a sheet of paper on the screen, which read 'not to be taken off for thirty days'. I lasted twenty days. On the twentieth day out of the thirty I watched a programme on my television. After this programme, I had to start the whole thirty-day process again.

This time I completed thirty days without watching television. I then took the sheet of paper off the screen and left the television there for a further fortnight. Not once did I turn it on. In my thirty days without it I had found other, more productive things to occupy my daily two hours with. I had broken the habit. I gave the television away and I have never had a TV since.

A habit I broke in a different way was smoking. This was in March 1988 when I was in the Air Force. One night I was sitting in the bar with my friends and I just pushed the box of 20 cigarettes into the centre of the table (I usually smoked between 20 and 25 a day) and announced in front of the seven other people sitting there,
"I've had my last cigarette, does anyone want these?"

You can imagine the industrial language that came flying back at me, but what I did here was make myself accountable to these people. My friends jokingly tried to get me to smoke again, presumably so they could ascertain how serious I was. However, because I was determined to keep the promise I had made to my friends, and myself; I successfully broke my habit beyond those thirty days, and since March 1988 I have never raised a cigarette to my mouth.

I am not sharing these two examples to try and impress you, or to try and state that I am someone special. Instead, I am trying to illustrate to you that habits can be created or broken as long as you have a desire to do what it takes to create or break them. Of course, sometimes it will be hard but it can be done. What is most important is that you need to find your own ways of putting the actions and methods into place, so that it becomes second nature to (for example) go for a three mile run every day before breakfast, or not to smoke.

The universe, by nature, always tries to fill a vacuum. This is no different for our minds and actions. Here is a thought for you: do not try to break a habit without filling the space it leaves with something. Why not aim to replace an unproductive habit with a productive habit? All successful people have productive habits. Furthermore, by filling the space left by unproductive habits with other things, it becomes much less effort to break these habits forever.

Our futures are determined by all of our habits, including the ones we think, speak, the actions we take and how we invest or spend our time. I would like to finish this section with this maxim that was written by an unknown author:

Be careful of your thoughts, for your thoughts become words.
Be careful of your words, for your words become actions.
Be careful of your actions, for your actions become habits.
Be careful of your habits, for your habits become your character.
Be careful of your character, for your character becomes your destiny.

It is Later Than you Think!

"Procrastination is the art of keeping up with yesterday" – Donald Marquis

Growth is required for things to progress in nature; and growth requires change. The people who move closer to their promises and objectives are those who recognise the requirement to change aspects of their life. This may involve anything from learning new skills, to changing their view of the world, to controlling their emotions. However, it is ultimately down to people taking the actions that they need to take, even when taking action is a risk and a leap of faith into an unknown territory.

The people who procrastinate tend to be those people who are risk averse, those who would rather that others assume the responsibility of taking risks. They avoid taking action so that if anything goes wrong they will also avoid being blamed. However, when nothing goes wrong and success is achieved for the people who have taken action, often the people who have procrastinated become envious and wish they had too taken this risk. These individuals may start to use phrases such as 'they are lucky', 'its all right for them', 'they have had it easy' 'they haven't had the problems I have had', and so on.

Does this sound like anyone you know? Their frustrations have become so great that they start to blame situational factors, and refuse to acknowledge that others have simply accepted responsibility, and to accept responsibility themselves.

So what causes people to procrastinate? There are many reasons, below are a list of some of the main ones. If you find that you relate to some of them, then I ask that you think seriously about how to take control, to set the change in motion and start to 'grow' past these feelings:

Fear
Not taking responsibility
External confusion
Disabilities
Depression
Wanting to escape
Pressures
Boredom
Dependent on others
Fatigue
Lack of clarity
Lack of confidence

Procrastinating is the behavioural equivalent of putting the brakes on. Once you acknowledge this, you can begin taking steps to move forward. No one wants to live with regrets and no one wants to say "if only". By following the steps and lessons in this book you can change your habits and your life for the better, for good. Start now, because life is short. **It is later than you think.**

So I encourage you to embrace the poem overleaf. The author unfortunately is unknown.

Do it Anyway

People are illogical, unreasonable, and self-centered
Love them anyway.
If you do good, people will accuse you of selfish ulterior motives.
Do good anyway.
If you are successful, you win false friends and true enemies.
Succeed anyway.
The good you do today will be forgotten tomorrow.
Do good anyway.
Honesty and frankness makes you vulnerable.
Be honest and frank anyway
The biggest people with the biggest ideas can be shot down by the smallest people with the smallest minds.
Think big anyway.
People favour underdogs but follow only top dogs.
Fight for a few underdogs anyway.
What you spend years building, may be destroyed over night.
Build anyway.
People really need help. but may attack you if you do help them.
Help them anyway.
Give the world the best you have and you'll get kicked in the teeth.
Give the world the best you have anyway.

Failure is a Great Teacher

"Failure is success if we learn from it" – Malcolm Forbes

Throughout the previous chapters we have talked about deciding what our model of success is, and set about taking some of the steps required to achieve what we want to achieve. However, for many of us the biggest thing holding us back is the fear of failure or rejection (as briefly mentioned in the chapter on emotions).

In reality, we will all have setbacks, mistakes and failures regardless of what we are doing. The nature of successful people is that when those inevitable setbacks occur, they simply dust themselves down and carry on, they do not let these setbacks stop them from achieving. These people, either consciously or subconsciously, will ask themselves:

"What lessons did I learn from that experience?"

It is often forgotten that when things go well, the path to success seems easy, but often our most important lessons come from the failures we face.

To adapt Malcolm Forbes' statement slightly:

"Failure is a great teacher if we are only willing to learn from it"

Why is this? It is because it is when setbacks occur that we should reflect, analyse, and work through the situation we may find ourselves in. It is these times that often we find out who we *really* are, and where our strengths lie.

"You show me someone who has never made a mistake and I will show someone who have never done anything" - Anonymous.

There are countless examples of people from all backgrounds and professions who faced obstacles and setbacks before they achieved their success. Here are a few notable stories:

Thomas Edison - American - inventor of the light bulb.

Edison had hundreds of attempts at creating what we now know as the 'light bulb', his father also labelled him a 'dunce'. After the successful invention of his light bulb, Edison was asked why he did not quit after so many failures. He pointed out that he did not consider them failures, just hundreds of examples of how not to make it work.

Sir Isaac Newton – Scientist – discovered many theories of physics including gravity.

Before discovering some of the theories that we take for granted today, Newton ran his family's farm. It was only after he was deemed a failure at running the farm that his was granted basic education allowance. Newton was placed in the bottom class because his teachers thought that he was not very bright.

Giacomo Puccini - famous Italian opera composer.

At the start of his passion for music, Puccini's music teacher thought he had no talent and refused to teach him.

Sir Richard Branson – entrepreneur

Sir Richard Branson almost went bankrupt and had to re-mortgage the family home to repay some of the bills, before he had success with his Virgin empire.

Colonel Sanders – the Colonel of KFC.

The Colonel had many people reject his recipe for Kentucky Fried Chicken before someone decided to give him a chance.

All of these individuals had to learn by their setbacks and failures in order to move towards their objectives. It may also be worth referring back to the stories of Albert Einstein, Evelyn Glennie, Helen Keller, Sir Winston Churchill, Sir Anthony Hopkins and Pablo Picasso in the chapter on belief. Similarly, all of these people will have had failures in the pursuit of their objectives, but will have implemented and learnt from the lessons they had learnt to move forward.

If you listen to successful people you will find that they do not refer to failure as failure, or mistakes as mistakes; rather they tend to be positive, and refer to them as learning experiences, diversions, opportunities to change direction and growth opportunities.

So what can we do to accept and learn from our setbacks? Well, we will start by changing the way we view these setbacks, and then by finding out what we can learn from them when they do happen.

As Norman Vincent Peale said:

"To change your circumstances, first start thinking differently"

The Only Constant is Change

"Grant me the serenity to accept the things I cannot change, the courage to change the things I can, and the wisdom to know the difference" – Francis of Assisi

When it comes to change you have two choices; change or be changed. Change around us is inevitable, so you should find ways to embrace change and ensure your actions work with it instead of against it.

As discussed in the chapter on habits, to change is not always easy. We may be in deeply embedded comfort zones through our habits, but it is possible.

A story:

It has been said that if a bullfrog were placed into boiling water, it would attempt to jump back out immediately. This is because the change in temperature would be too severe for it to deal with at once. However, if you were to put this frog in lukewarm water and slowly heat the water up, it would stay there until it was boiled to death. This is because the change would be so subtle and slow that it would not realise that the water was too hot.

The principle of the story is '*change, or be changed*', this bullfrog firstly tried to change its environment by trying to jump out. In the second scenario it waited to be changed, by which time it was too late.

As identified in Francis of Assisi's words: you need to identify what you can and should change, and recognise the things you cannot and should not change. To progress with the promises that you have made for yourself, you must make sure that you change what you need to change, for the better.

Nature gives us many examples of creatures changing their form to fit in with their environment. This is based on the 'survival of the fittest' premise, as creatures in nature often have to change just to survive, or they would end up being eaten by their predators. Fortunately for us, the consequences of not embracing change would, in most cases, not have such fatal results, but it could limit our success and halt our progress in achieving what we want out of life.

Change is inevitable and unavoidable, and we do not have control over every aspect of it. The determining factor in how we see change is whether we react or respond to it. So I ask you this: how you deal with change? Do you see it as an opportunity or as a burden? This decision is yours to make.

The type of change you can control one hundred percent of the time is internal change. This may include aspects of your life such as diet, habits, attitude, life style and self-development, to name but a few.

If you think that you do not have sufficient time to make changes, as many of us do, then I will share a thought with you. 'Time' is merely a suitcase of 24 hours. Everyone here has exactly the same size suitcase. There are people who achieve a lot in their 24 hours, and there are people who achieve very little. The only difference between these people is how well they 'pack' that suitcase. It really is that simple.

There is a simple change that we can all do, that will give you more time, and the change is a very small change. Are you ready? *Get out of bed half an hour earlier each day for six days a week every week of the year.* This will give you an extra three hours a week, and over the year you will have increased your productive time by 156 hours. Think what could you achieve with this extra time. Just a few ideas include reading a self development or educational book, listening to an audio programme, doing some exercise, spending quality time with your loved ones, the list is almost endless. All I ask is that you make sure this time is spent doing something productive.

Have you got into the habit of staying in bed longer than you need? If so, this challenge may prove difficult. Bill Cullen was the man who turned Renault Ireland, which was running at a $20 million loss, into a very profitable company with an annual turnover of $350 million. In his book "Golden Apples" shares something that his Grandmother Molly Darcy, who lived until she was 100, told him - something that may help you make that adjustment:

"Sleeping is the nearest thing to dying you'll ever do, so don't do too much of it".

The Power of Self-Development

"Don't let your schooling get in the way of your education" – Mark Twain

It is a sad occurrence when people, for one reason or another, stop reading educational books and continuing to learn once they leave school, college or university. These institutions teach us many useful theories and insights but they do not always show us how to implement the education we have acquired to achieve our targets. We learn that through what I call the 'University of Life".

Some people simply stop reading or listening to things that help them grow and develop their imagination and minds. Instead they start watching television, reading newspapers, fictional books and magazines of various sorts. At best, these provide escapism and light relief, and at worst gradually convince and condition individuals into believing that the world is a negative place, with no hope of them achieving anything.

Now let me make it quite clear: there is nothing wrong with watching television, reading newspapers or reading fictional books from time to time, if that is what you want to do. All that I am suggesting is that we can perhaps replace some of this by giving time to other types of reading and listening, particularly in the field of self-development.

The power of self-development should not be underestimated. Those who have achieved what they really wanted to have all understood the power of self-development, and they actively seek out where they can get the information they require.

Self-development means much more than acquiring qualifications. It concerns the growth, development and change of the person from the inside. This is where one of the challenges lies for many. Some people struggle to engage with it, possibly because the changes do not happen overnight. Once again, it is focus on small, incremental changes that mean improvement and progression is constant.

Another challenge is that people, by nature, do not like change. As discussed, we must change in order to grow and develop into the best and most successful people we can become; yet so many people avoid actively pursuing self-development activities.

We currently live in a culture that is largely driven by immediate gratification, i.e. the notion that 'we must have it now'. This is evident with quick-fix weight loss programmes, internet shopping promising next day delivery, and the rise in social media communication, to name but a few influencing factors. Information is available more readily and attention spans are shorter. The natural process of self-development does not work in the same way, so often people are discouraged when they do not see immediate results and they give up.

The overriding key to self-development lies in our ability to continue learning, reading, listening, attaining these new skills (in whatever form they may come) and staying persistent, even though we may not see results straight away.

It will take time, and in some cases change can take years. The changes can be subtle to the point that we do not even notice them happening. Then, all of a sudden, we start achieving more than we ever thought possible. This is because we will have adapted into the person we needed to be in order to achieve the desired results.

In my workshops I often state the following:

"*If we want the answers just observe nature, because the answers are there – there is nothing new under the sun*".

Nature gives us many excellent examples of the principle of constant and persistent action with amazing results, despite nothing appearing to alter over a period of years. Let me share this narrative with you:

The Chinese Bamboo Tree of Indonesia starts life off as a seed. Like all seeds it has to be nurtured with water, fertile soil and sunshine on a consistent basis. In the first year nothing happens, we do not witness any visible alterations below or above the surface of the soil.

During the second year we continue to nurture the seed by feeding it with water, ensuring the soil is fertile, keeping it in the sunlight, and yet there are still no visible signs of growth.

All the way through the third year we make the same progress and yet still see the same results: no visible growth. Think how frustrated would we become with no visible results. Would we even continue?

Four years after we planted the seed we still have seen no growth, despite continuing all the required actions. Would you have given up on the seed by now? Most people would.

In the fifth year, because of the continuous nurturing of the seed through watering, fertile soil and sun; something amazing happens. Sometime in this fifth year a small sprout appears, then within six weeks of this sprout appearing, the plant grows by ninety feet.

The question here is, did the bamboo tree grow ninety feet in six weeks, or it take five years of nurturing and developing, despite having no visible results, in preparation for the sudden growth that it experiences. The answer is that of course, it took five years not six weeks.

This analogy shows how our lives are often similar to that of the bamboo tree. Whilst for the bamboo tree's development it needed water, fertile soil and sun, for our own development we may need tools such as books, audio programmes and seminars, amongst a positive attitude and clear targets and being focused on what we want to achieve.

Waiting for visible results can be very frustrating and discouraging, particularly because we may be working constantly and yet not be receiving the outcomes and rewards we think we should. However, for those individuals who are persistent and do not allow themselves to become discouraged, positive changes will start to happen.

So how do you gather the self-development information that will help us development and grow? Well, there are simply hundreds of resources available if you just search for them. Self-development works on the premise that we are ultimately our own teachers as well as students. Some of the information we come across will not be relevant to our current situation, but further down our journey it may become relevant. Also you will find that you prefer some authors to others, which is great. To this I would encourage you to enjoy the authors who you can relate to and learn from them.

Some popular resources are books, audio programmes, workshops and seminars. You can also get some very good resources from the internet, but be selective. Find yourself a mentor or coach and put time into networking in the fields that you want to develop. This can also reap great benefits.

Persistence is Omnipotent

"Persistence is the hard work you do after you get tired of doing the hard work you already did" – Mewt Gingrich

The importance of persistence is often underestimated and overlooked. In truth, this attribute should be of paramount importance in your quest towards your goals.

Persistence is not glamorous: it combines all of the work that you carry out in the background that others rarely see. In a world where people expect instant gratification and rewards, many fail to realise that they are expected to keep on going when they encounter setbacks. Without persistence, people struggle to attain what they want in life; they give up too early or too easily.

I can guarantee that every person that I have mentioned in this book had to be extremely persistent to achieve what he or she did.

Having sincere passion and enthusiasm for what you are trying to achieve are huge factors that will help to develop your persistence. Many people confuse passion with enthusiasm when in fact; enthusiasm comes from passion. Passion operates on the principle that regardless of someone's (absence of) skills, education and opportunities, the individual in question will do everything in their power to complete the job in hand.

Enthusiasm, on the other hand, is a by-product of passion and is what will drive the project forward when times get difficult. It is here that the trait of persistence will emerge.

It is worth bearing in mind that many leaders in various industries and businesses have said that they would be willing to pay over the odds to hire someone with passion and persistence, as opposed someone with only ability. This principle is backed up in the following poem written by Calvin Coolidge:

Persistence

"Nothing in the world can take the place of persistence
Talent will not; nothing is more common than unsuccessful men with talent
Genius will not; unrewarded genius is almost a proverb
Education will not; the world is full of educated derelicts
Persistence and determination alone are omnipotent.

To be persistent when we are working towards our goals takes discipline. In fact, every 'success' that has been mentioned in this book has required discipline.

Please now work through the exercise overleaf. This exercise is designed to establish where you should focus your efforts, in order to obtain the discipline required to attain the promises you have made to yourself.

Do this exercise without input from others, as you know yourself better than anyone.

1) Broadly summarise the three areas of your life in which you feel you need more discipline.

____

____

____

2) List them in the order of their importance, starting with the most important.

____

____

____

3) There are many resources available that can help with motivation, instruction and information on the areas you have selected, but remember that in order to be motivated, you must have a real desire for this change.

4) Find a mentor who is willing to hold you accountable. Ensure that they possess in themselves the disciplines you want to work on, and they are someone you respect. Be considerate to your mentor and do not abuse their kindness.

5) Spend some time every day planning what you going to work on (many people do this last thing at night ready for the following day). This should take around 30 minutes. Then spend the rest of the day carrying out the actions in the plan. It is better to do a little towards your goals every day than a lot in one go infrequently. The important thing is to ensure do you something that will move you forward.

6) These changes do not happen overnight, give yourself at least between 30-90 days to see a change. You must be both patient and persistent.

7) Once you have achieved the discipline you want then reward yourself, and share it with your mentor. This does not need to be anything big; it can be something like watching your favourite film, a daytrip somewhere nice, a new pair of shoes, or anything you consider to be a reward.

Persistence comes from discipline. The key message is that we all have to do things that we don't necessarily want to do from time to time. In reality, the people who move forward are those who do what has to be done and not only the things that they want to do.

Is Good Enough Really Good Enough?

"We are what we repeatedly do. Excellence, then, is not an act, but a habit" – Aristotle

"Oh that will do, that's good enough".

Does that phrase sound familiar? How many times have you said that or something similar to yourself when doing a task? We are probably all guilty of it sometimes. But, in those times, can you honestly say that you really did do the best that you could have done, or did you sell yourself shorter than what you could have accomplished?

I would like to stress here that I am **not** talking about perfection. The practice of waiting for a time, environment or situation to be perfect can have an adverse effect on our productivity, and can often hold us back simply because 'the perfect time' will never actually exist. There will always be something not quite right, so if we wait for the perfect time then we will have a very long wait.

In essence, "good enough" is not, quite frankly, good enough. Rather, doing your best and giving a task the most effort you can give is good enough.

The sports arena demonstrates this principle. Often, coaches of teams will select their team using the players who give 100%. They will not select the players who will only give 75% effort, even though these people may indeed be more talented than the ones who give 100%.

Why might this be the case? It is because people, particularly during competitions, are expected to give only the best, which means putting in all of the effort that they can for the entire duration of the day, or match. For someone to make this much effort demonstrates that they are fully committed. Hence, anyone who does not put in all of his or her effort is not fully committed.

The principles of effort and commitment are directly linked to our attitude, and it is these principles that help us achieve what we most desire in our lives.

It is a sad fact that many people have a "that'll do" attitude, and these individuals will make the minimum amount of effort required and not use their talents to their fullest. In short: they will not go the *extra mile*. The people who really achieve what they want are the people who do go the extra mile.

The head engineer of NASA's research and development team, Warner Von Braun, set extremely high standards and believed only the best would ever be acceptable. When discussing the Saturn V Rocket, Von Braun said the following:

"The Saturn V has 5,600,000 parts. Even if we had a 99% reliability, there would still be 5,600 defective parts. Yet, the Apollo IV mission flew a textbook flight with only two anomalies occurring, demonstrating a reliability of 99.999%. If an average automobile with 13,000 parts were to have the same reliability, it would have its first defective part in about a hundred years."

The above shows very well what can be achieved if only we all go the 'extra mile' and set higher than average standards. We can achieve great things when we have the attitude that "good enough is not good enough, only the best is good enough".

However, this has to be done consciously and purposefully, because humans are designed to take the route of least resistance. Many people allow themselves to take this route; and they do not tend to achieve what they want or could have in life. Make sure that you don't fall into this trap and be warned; heading towards the route with the least resistance is something that tends to creep up on us if we do not make the decision not to let it.

During my time in the Royal Air Force, I found myself reading a Dutch Flight Safety Magazine. Upon reading and being impressed by a poem in the magazine, I wrote it down so I could remember it. It was not until I was collating material for this book that I came across my scribbles, which I feel describe this section of the book very aptly.

"Good Enough"

My friend, beware of 'good enough'
It isn't made of sterling stuff
It's something anyone can do
It marks the many from the few
It has no merit to the eye
It's something any one can buy
Its name but a sham and bluff

For it is never 'good enough'.

With 'good enough' the shirkers stop
In any factory, shop or any work
With 'good enough' the shirkers rest and lose
To those who give their best
With 'good enough' the plane breaks down
And we fall short of high renown
My friend, remember, and be wise,
In 'good enough' disaster lies.

With 'good enough' have many ships been wrecked
The forward march of armies checked
Great buildings burned and fortunes lost
How can the world compute the cost?
In life and money it has been paid
Because of 'good enough' we stayed
Who stops at 'good enough' shall find success
Has left them behind.

There is no 'good enough', that's short of what you can do,
And you ought.
The flaw that may escape the eye and temporarily get by
Shall weaken underneath the strain, and wreck
The ship, car or plane.
For this is true; you should not bluff...
ONLY THE BEST IS GOOD ENOUGH

The bottom line is this that the principle of 'only the best is good enough' can be broken down to three words:

striving for excellence. Therefore, make excellence a habit by striving for it in every thing you do.

Know your Behavioural Quadrant

"Human behaviour is both a science and an art. As a science it can be studied and understood, as an art it can be acted upon and adapted" – John Borthwick

This chapter involves taking a brief look at behaviour profiling. If you are better aware of your own personality and behavioural traits, you will be better equipped to make the adaptations you require to achieve excellence in your goals and personal promises.

Our behaviour drives everything we do, and despite the fact that we are all different; we are also all *predictably* different. So how can you use this to help achieve what you want to?

Before I explain what I mean by 'predictably' different, I need to stress that this chapter is simply an overview of the main elements of DISC profiling, it is not within the scope of this book to go into any great detail. Also, the methods of DISC profiling are not about pigeonholing people, particularly as people are a 'blend' or 'mix' of what I am about to cover.

Ever since humans first appeared on earth they have been fascinated with the behaviour and personality of other humans, including understanding why they do what they do. Each and every one of your thought-processes, preferences and environment affect your behaviour. Your behaviour, in turn, shapes your personality. Your personality is also shaped by hereditary factors, experiences you had after the age of 8, and any role models you had before the age of 12. Hence you can see why no two people are the same.

A long time ago, there were believed to be four main (core) behavioural quadrants and a number of mixes (blends) of these four quadrants. In 444BC Empedocles called them earth, air, fire and water. In 400BC Hippocrates called them choleric, sanguine, phlegmatic and melancholy. Then in 1921 Jung renamed then thinking, feeling, sensation and intuition.

In 1928 William Moulton Marston PhD wrote a book entitled 'Emotions of Normal People'. In this he described the core quadrants as Dominance, Influence, Steadiness and Compliance, which then became known as the DISC Model.

The DISC model is a positive tool and can be used to help people identify and make effective use of their strengths. At the same time it can help people identify their 'blind spots' and potential weaknesses, which may be areas to work on to help them move towards their objectives.

It is worth pointing out here that there are no better, worse, right or wrong blends, they are simply different - predictably different. I should also say that these 'blind spots' or weaknesses are really just our strengths taken too far or overused.

People with different blends of personality can and do achieve great accomplishments. There is no reason for anyone not to use their natural talents to move towards the promises they make to themselves. To do this, everyone must understand the principles of motivation, which are as follows:

1) You cannot be motivated by others alone; it is an inside job.

2) People are motivated by their own reasons to do something, not by someone else's reasons.

3) Communication is enhanced and greatly improved by having an understanding of behavioural styles.

4) Instinctively we tend to move away from our fears to an environment that is more comfortable (namely, our core behavioural quadrant).

By having an understanding of the DISC model and your own behavioural blend, you can adapt to whichever environment you find yourself in by adapting your behaviour. This may be within networking in business, office politics, family situations, corporate events and social occasions within your community or friendship group.

Understanding the DISC model can also help to reduce your stress levels and better handle conflict. Essentially, it will help you to appreciate the differences of other people and ultimately have a positive effect on your relationships. DISC works on the premise that to understand others', we first need to understand ourselves. Through this understanding we are empowered to adopt our behaviour when required.

There have been an abundance of research reports on the subject of human behaviour and the effect it has on the 'success' of the individual. The general consensus is that the amount of success that someone has is more accountable to their communication skills and quality of their interaction with other humans, than their technical ability, knowledge or education.

Please refer to appendix 1 for a simple overview of the traits of the 'core' quadrants. I would also advice that you invest in identifying your own core quadrant by having your profile administered by a trained professional.

Do you Listen to Your Self-Talk?

"Your mind believes everything it is told, positive or negative. Make sure it is positive because it does not discriminate" – Anonymous.

The brain has an amazing ability: it registers everything that it is told. Your brain will repeat and focus on the information it hears most, on a subconscious level. It does not differentiate between tone and attitude.

So if you constantly tell yourself that you are no good at something, soon enough your brain will start to believe it. On the other hand, if you consistently tell it that you are good at something, soon enough it will start believing that too. That is why your self-talk is so important to the attainment of your objectives, because you are effectively 'programming' yourself for success or failure.

Let us take an example: the media. Television programmes and newspapers tend to focus on negative stories. Many people spend hours in front of their TV watching a variety of material without considering the effect it is having on their brains. Humans tend to think in pictures rather than words, so by watching television and looking at horrifying pictures in newspapers our minds are being 'programmed' effectively by the media.

I will ask you take a moment to consider why marketing companies spend extremely large amounts of money on 30-second commercial adverts, to be shown on prime time television during peak hours. These companies are fully aware of the effect that repeated viewing has on people's brains, which is why they have chosen to spend that money.

It is exactly the same principle as that of self-talk. Positive self-talking is so powerful that it affects our minds by 'programming' what our perception of life is. Ultimately, it can help us formulate our habits, which formulate our actions.

The best way to change this is by being aware of the negative statements you say to yourself, and trying to do this less often. Try to change these statements to positive ones, and start talking to yourself with an optimistic and positive frame of mind, thus programming the best computer that nature has ever devised – your brain.

Your brain, as stated above, will start believing the positive things and will get to work on making these things happen. Your own thought processes then start to become part of the solution instead of the problem. It takes time and effort for this habit to change, but it will.

It is also true that people are naturally more attracted to people with a positive outlook on life than those with a negative outlook, which may just work in your favour!

To help the positive programming of your mind, exploit the power of visualisation. Visualising success will help to keep you on track and stay enthused. It is a little-known fact that the brain cannot distinguish between feelings of actual success and feelings of imagined success.

Remembering what you are passionate about and why you are striving to achieve your goals will go a long way to helping you to maintain the enthusiasm needed to complete them.

So start running a mental film of what your model of success looks like in your mind's eye, and run it time and time again. This will help your mind to start focusing and finding ways, ideas, and solutions to help you move you forward to your goals.

As with all good things, this takes time. It does not and will not happen overnight. Your mind may take time to erase or alter the negative thought-processes that it is used to. Be patient and persistent and you will start to see results.

I had to go through this process for a long time before I had the courage and confidence to go for a London Academy of Music and Dramatic Art (LAMDA) Gold Medal in Public Speaking. I was struggling with my beliefs based on my past (which I have already shared with you). Furthermore I had to keep reminding myself what Mr Millet told me at school all those years ago. Finally, I kept that promise to myself; I practiced visualising myself doing my speeches and I gained my gold medal in the year 2000.

The 'Garcia' Effect

"The most delightful surprise in life is to recognize your own worth" – Maxwell Maltz

In the late 1800's an event happened that was to produce a 'filler' article in a small American newspaper named The Philistine. This article was written by someone called Elbert Hubbard, and was soon to become one of the most reproduced pieces of literature ever written.

I would like to share with you the story how this article came about: Elbert Hubbard was having dinner with his family and they were debating who was the overriding hero of the Spanish/Cuban war. They pondered over whether it was Garcia, who was president of Cuba at the time, or McKinley who was the President of the USA. Hubbard's son said he disagreed with both, and that in fact a man named Rowan was the indirect hero of the Spanish/Cuban war because he carried out a task that was to change the outcome of this conflict. Hubbard realised that his son was right. He jumped up from the dinner table and immediately wrote an article, which would later be placed in an American newspaper as the filler article.

Andrew Summers Rowan was an Officer in the USA Army at the time of the Spanish/Cuban war. President McKinley asked his Generals if there was someone who could get a message to President Garcia asking what support he needed, the Generals unanimously said that Rowan could do it. President McKinley gave Rowan this instruction, to which Rowan said 'yes', and three weeks later he returned to McKinley with his reply from Garcia.

When instructed to carry out this task, Rowan did not ask any further questions regarding whom he should contact, their location, or how he would deliver the message. Rowan simply carried out what was asked of him. In doing this he proved that he could carry out a task without giving up, without asking others to think for him, and without asking others to make decisions on his behalf. Despite the situation being unfavourable towards him, Rowan took responsibility for the outcome of the task ahead. Ultimately, he resolved to get the job done whatever it took.

Today, people are too willing to let others do their thinking for them. They let other people take responsibility for them and their lives, and allow others to control their futures. What we need is more 'Rowans'. Are you a Rowan?

Leaders in business often say that the following article, written by Elbert Hubbard, is one of the greatest lessons ever produced because it's powerful message about taking the initiative, completing an instruction and getting a job done with minimal fuss.

When the article was first published Hubbard received a handful of requests for copies, then hundreds of requests, then thousands, then hundreds of thousands. The Russian Railway Company wanted a copy for all employees, then the Japanese Mikado of Japan at the time wanted a copy for every member of the Japanese army. The magazine East Aurora, issued on 1st December 1913 quoted that in 14 years some 40 million copies of this article were in print.

So what could be so stirring, moving and inspiring about this article that so many copies would be printed in such a short period of time, particularly considering the printing technology back then? I would like to share two passages from this article – and note that what is also amazing about this article is that you would never know it was written in the 1800s.

The point I wish to make is this: McKinley gave Rowan a letter to be delivered to Garcia. Rowan took the letter and did not ask, "Where is he at? "By the eternal, there is a man whose form should be cast in deathless bronze and the statue placed in every college in the land. It is not book-learning young people need, nor instruction about this and that, but a stiffening of the vertebrae which will cause them to be loyal to a trust, to act promptly, concentrate their energies: do the thing, "Carry a message to Garcia"... You reader: put this matter to a test. You are sitting now in your office. Six clerks are within call. Summon any one and make this request: "Please look in the encyclopaedia and make a brief memorandum for me concerning the life of Correggio." Will the clerk quietly say, "Yes," and go do the task. On your life they will not. They will look at you out of a fishy eye and ask one or more of the following questions: Who is it? Which encyclopaedia? Where is the encyclopaedia? Was I hired for that? Don't you mean Bismarck? What's the matter with Charlie doing it? Is he dead? Is there any hurry? Shan't I bring the book and let you look it up yourself? What do you want to know for?... Now if you are wise you will not bother to explain to your assistant that Correggio is indexed under the C's and not under the K's, but you will smile sweetly and say "never mind'" and go look it up yourself..."

Does this sound familiar to you today? Things have not really changed in the last 100 years have they? Hubbard continues:

"*We have recently been hearing much maudlin sympathy expressed for the downtrodden denizen of the sweatshop and the homeless wanderer searching for honest employment and with it all often go many hard words for the people in power. Nothing is said about the employer who grows old before their time in a vain attempt to get frowsy ne'er-do-wells to do intelligent work; and their long patient striving with "help" that does nothing but loaf when their back is turned...Have I put the matter too strongly? Possibly I have, but when all the world has gone a–summing, I wish to speak a word of sympathy for the person who succeeds... my heart goes out to the person who does their work when the boss is away as well as when they are at home. And the person, who, when given a letter for Garcia, quietly takes the missive, without asking any idiotic questions, and with no lurking intention of chucking it into the nearest sewer, or of doing anything else but deliver it, never gets laid off, nor has to go on strike for higher wages. Civilisation is one long anxious search for such individuals. Anything such a person asks shell be granted. Their kind are so rare that no employer can afford to let them go. They are wanted in every city, town, and village; in every office, shop, store and factory. The world cries out for such. They are needed and needed badly, the person who can carry a message to Garcia."*

This message to Garcia, as I see it, symbolises the things that we want to achieve for ourselves, and the promises that we have made ourselves. The journey of a message from McKinley to Garcia was no easy one, but someone took full responsibility for making it happen. If I were to give you a message to take to your Garcia, could you do it with no further questions and minimal fuss, just as Rowan did? I believe quite passionately that the answer to that question should be yes!

Thomas Edison once said that success is 5% inspiration and 95% perspiration. So become a Rowan: adopt his spirit and determination and deliver the message to 'your' Garcia.

It's Time to Choose

"One never knows what they might accomplish until they try. That is so simple that some people completely overlook it" Ric De Vos

What I hope I have illustrated in this small book is that it really does not matter what background you are from, what education you have, what challenges you have faced, where you live or what experiences you have had that determine if you achieve what your model of success is. Granted, the factors that I have just mentioned may influence how you perceive the world around you, but they do not determine what happens and the results you have. That is an inside job.

You have the ability to choose and make decisions about where you want to go and achieve in life. Anthony Robbins once said:

"It's in the moments of decision that you shape your destiny".

This sentence highlights that the decisions we make, regardless of how large or small they seem, when combined with others over a period of time will all have an effect in the future. There is one universal principle that nature has that will ensure this will happen and that is the golden rule of 'cause and effect'.

It is all down to the focus, beliefs, attitudes, actions and responses that we practise, as well as how persistent we are with these. Everything that happens to you is a neutral experience; it is your choice whether you perceive individual experiences as good or bad. To put it another, perhaps more famous way: is the glass half full or is it half empty? That decision is yours.

As you work towards the goals or promises you have made, remember the principles outlined above. As Winston Churchill said to students at an American university: *"Never give up, never, never give up"*.

Along your journey you will almost certainly come across critics who will challenge what you are working towards. These critics will inadvertently (or deliberately) try to get you to break the goals or promises you have made to yourself. When this happens, I ask you to think of the following passage, said by Theodore Roosevelt when he was US president:

"It is not the critic who counts: not the man who points out when the strong man stumbles, or where the doer of deeds could have done them better. The credit belongs to the man who is actually in the arena, whose face is marred by dust and sweat and blood, who strives valiantly: who errs and comes short again and again; because there is not effect without error and shortcomings; but who does actually strive to do the deed; who knows the great enthusiasm, the great devotion, who spends himself in a worthy cause, who at the best knows in the end the triumph of high achievement and who at the worst, if he fails, at least he fails whilst daring greatly. So that his place shall never be with those cold and timid souls who know neither victory nor defeat."

I would like to leave you the following that I came across a number of years ago. Unfortunately I have not found out who the author is but I thought it was so powerful and true I would like to share it with you:

Success is the result of caring more than others think is wise;
Risking more than others think is safe;
Dreaming more than others think is practical and expecting more than others think is possible.

I was once talking to someone who said something to me that I have remembered ever since. It is not meant to scare you, rather highlight a point. He asked me what year was I born and I told him. This man then told me that there would, one day, be a line between that date and the date that I die on a head stone or somewhere, no one ever knows how 'long' that line will be. He then explained that the only thing that really matters is what you do between the beginning and the end of that line, and that is what defines you from others. What he meant was that most people just *let* life happen to them. Very few *decide* what will happen to them.

Keep a date with the goals and promises you have made for yourself, and remember this, **that if you think you have exhausted all options: you have not.** You deserve to keep your goals and promises and to achieve them. As Les Brown said:

"*it's not over until you win*".

The goals and promises you have made are all within your reach; go for them and never give up. Always remember that you are travelling along that line and that:

"It's later than you think!"

Appendices

Appendix one

Below is a short overview of the key traits of the 4 DISC 'behavioural' or 'personality' quadrants. To obtain an effective and working understanding of these traits, how the blends work with each other, and to achieve better interaction between yourself and others, it is strongly recommended you complete a profile.

A HIGH 'D' INTENSITY

Core motivation:

These people require challenge, control and choices.

Their preferred environment:

High D's like to have freedom, activities that are varied and tasks that challenge them. They like authority and opportunities that will give them the chance of advancement.

People who they respond best to are:

Those who will stick to business and give direct answers, strive under pressure, set clear goals to achieve and who give 'freedom' for personal accomplishments.

Possible development areas:

High D's should recognise that they are allowed to relax, that people are important, that they are accountable to someone, that there needs to be some controls and that they may need to verbalise conclusions in a way that others can understand better.

A HIGH 'I' INTENSITY

Core motivation:

These people need to feel they are popular with everyone, that they have recognition and approval.

Their preferred environment:

High I's like to verbalise their ideas and have the opportunity to influence and inspire others. They like to have prestige, and have friendly relationships.

People who they respond best to:

Those who will give the high I the recognition for their abilities that they crave, people who are involved in social opportunities outside work, those who create an exciting atmosphere and those who provide incentives for those wanting to take risks.

Possible development areas:

High I's may need to learn the importance of listening and realise that time management is imperative; that once they have started a task it needs to be completed.

Their over-optimism may sometimes have an adverse effect.

A HIGH 'S' INTENSITY

Core motivation:

These people need to have assurance, security and appreciation.

Their preferred environment:

High S's like to have a work pattern that is established, they like to stabilise situations, and feel most comfortable within consistent environments that they can identify with.

People who they respond best to:

High S's respond best to those who are relaxed and who allow them the time to adjust and adapt with changing surroundings. This allows them to work at their own pace without feeling rushed. They also enjoy being given clear defined objectives and the means to complete them.

Possible development areas:

These people may need to accept that change can be a good thing, that discipline is sometimes required and can be positive. They may need reminding that it is not a crime to say 'no' from time to time and that friendship is not always everything.

A HIGH 'C' INTENSITY

Core Motivation:

These people want excellence, value and quality answers in everything they do.

Their Preferred Environment:

A high C likes to have the time and resources to complete tasks, which have been clearly defined and explained fully with all the necessary details. They do not like to be exposed to high risks, and team participation is something they enjoy. High C's will meticulously plan all of the jobs allocated to them.

People who they respond best to:

High C's require an open-door policy, with people who will give assurance and create a supportive atmosphere. They also like people to provide as much detail as positive, with defined operating parameters.

Possible Development Areas:

These individuals may need to realise that deadlines are important and need to be met. It is not always possible to maintain such a high level of detail in everything they do. They may require assistance in feeling that taking a calculated risk can be productive. A high C may feel uncomfortable when total support is not possible, and they may need guidance understanding that there are varying degrees of excellence.

* 9 7 8 1 7 8 0 3 5 2 9 4 7 *

ND - #0191 - 060826 - C0 - 210/148/8 - PB - 9781780352947 - Gloss Lamination